D1233407

Volume 70 of the Yale Series of Younger Poets

Snow on Snow

MAURA STANTON

Foreword by Stanley Kunitz

YALE UNIVERSITY PRESS, NEW HAVEN AND LONDON, 1975

Published with assistance from
The Mary Cady Tew Memorial Fund.

Library of Congress catalog card number: 74-21349
International standard book number: 0-300-01866-5 (cloth)
0-300-01867-3 (paper)

Designed by Sally Sullivan
and set in Monotype Aldine Bembo type.
Printed in the United States of America.

Published in Great Britain, Europe, and Africa by
Yale University Press, Ltd., London.
Distributed in Latin America by Kaiman & Polon,
Inc., New York City; in Australasia and Southeast
Asia by John Wiley & Sons Australasia Pty. Ltd.,
Sydney; in India by UBS Publishers' Distributors Pvt.,
Ltd., Delhi; in Japan by John Weatherhill, Inc., Tokyo.

For Richard

Contents

III

Acknowledgments

Acknowledgment is made to the following publications for poems that originally appeared in them.

The American Poetry Review: "The All-Night Waitress," "Autobiography," "The Conjurer," "Ophelia," "Short Story," "The Snow House," "Caring for the Generals"

The American Review: "Lovers Leaving My Bed"

The Ark River Review: "Dreaming of Shells," "Judith Recalls Holofernes"

Eating the Menu: Contemporary American Poetry 1963–1973: "The Boy Next Door: A Pastoral," "The Fisherman's Wife"

The Iowa Review: "In Ignorant Cadence"

The Midwest Quarterly: "Elegy for the Whole Ward"

The New York Quarterly: "Letter to Kafka"

Poetry: "The Dreams," "The Sled"

Poetry Northwest: "Going Back"

Poetry Now: "In the House of the Brain," "North," "The Stutterer"

Shaman: "Mykonos," "Barnyard"

Shenandoah: "Perspectives," "Widows"

Special thanks to Dr. Bernard Coan.

Foreword

Maura Stanton's poetry does not lend itself to easy definition. In the elusiveness of her themes, in her rejection of concepts, in her flow of metaphor, in her musical structuring, she seems to be aiming at the condition of an absolute art, a "pure poetry," as first defined by Poe. From my understanding of her objectives, if you were to ask her what she is saying in any of her poems, her reply would have to be in the form of another poem. And if you were to beg her to describe the reality extrapolated in her metaphors, she would have to tell you that what she sees as metaphor is what she knows as real. Her work manifestly embraces such an aesthetic, but without the slightest trace of dogma. She would be inclined, I suspect, to agree with Valéry's somewhat tardy recognition that, given the nature of language, "pure poetry" is at best a phantom goal, only intermittently attainable, since sound and sense, image and idea are no less indissolubly wedded than body and soul.

Because of the lyric intensity and complex tissue of her work, we are not likely to think of Maura Stanton as a dramatic poet, but indeed many of her poems break from an episodic node and proceed along a tenuous line of action, through which dreams and memories shuttle. In "Perceptions" she opens with the recollection of one night in her Midwest childhood when she plodded from door to door, selling Christmas seals, gold stamps "with egg-white angels / trumpeting askew in the trees." We are not handed her feelings on a platter, but some of the details—the "blunt wind" scouring her eyes, the Christmas lights "strung in ersatz steeples," the dog moving "wolflike" over the front-yard crèche—hint that we would be wrong to anticipate a sentimental reverie. In the next flash—"years later"—we see her burning to ash a seal that she has found curled in the crack of a bureau drawer. As the fire begins to consume this relic from her past, a totally unexpected but compelling ant clambers "furiously from the smoke / with a huge bread crumb / lodged in his black jaw"—another refugee from eternity. The concluding lines, bringing past and present luminously together, fusing all the ingredients that have gone into the making of the poem, fairly leap off the page in a blast of images:

> Somehow today, squinting
> at a file of ants on a leaf—
> they're inscrutable as cuneiform.
> I believed death was simply
> bone against bone, thoughtlessness—
> the way a crushed ant dries
> & blows through the grass
> without memory or direction.
> What were angels but wishes?
> Now their pellucid wings
> loom in my dreams. I see
> the real meaning of trumpets
> & that fierce gift, not death,
> but the tumult of perception.

In another poem, "The Sled," the jolt up her spine shaft at the end of a downhill coast onto a frozen lake reawakens her early trauma of paralysis in an iron lung. She observes her husband waving to her from the top of the hill and thinks of his fingers at night tracing the snaking curve of her spine.

> I remember polio: braces, hooks, machines
> shiny as sled runners, the wool packs
> steaming my body like a snowman's.

His ministering hand is like a doctor's, restraining the death wish, the desire "to fly / toward the lake until ice breaks me." As in so many of Maura Stanton's poems, but here more palpably than usual, the tension of the dialectic hints at a psychic battleground where Eros and Thanatos contend for overlordship. The lines gather speed and confidence as they approach their destination:

> A survivor has white lips sucking
> her brain, all those other beds
> crammed with nervous children in gowns
> who tumble forever in snowlight
> unable to stand. Once more downhill
> together, his arms saying alive! alive!
> we lean from the lake & keep going.

The snow is forever falling in the country of Maura Stanton's imagination, as it must have seemed to fall in Peoria and Minneapolis, the places of her childhood. Only the silent, the lonely, and the lost fit snugly into that white landscape. The snowpack waits to smother the living: "If the sheet stays warm/ for half-an-hour, why do I dream/ avalanche!" Someone by whom she felt rejected years ago emerges as "the man who mailed me snow." When, in an adult tantrum, she is tempted to destroy her neighbors' children's igloo, she refrains from doing so:

> If I kicked their snow house into snow,
> paradoxically I'd return each night
> to build it up, flake by flake ...

The snow prairie, in its remorseless beauty, suggestive of the classic ideal of perfection, is internalized as the prescience of a stillness to be laid on the heart; while the howling blizzard, piling snow on snow, speaks to her of the fury of existence.

As soon as the snow is driven from one of Maura Stanton's poems, images of stone and bone and salt and shell rush in to take its place. White is her universal color, often in a most surprising context. "Do you understand," she asks, in her poem addressed to Kafka, "how I need your white sperm?"

> If you mumble about your father
> what can I say? Here is mine—

> a whole childhood of frown and circumference
> locked on a prairie without a history,
> without oracular words like "Prague" or "Jew."
> Of course you want nothing from me. You are salt.
> You fly in my wounds when I wake up
> blind in the darkness, calling for a thesaurus
> to explain sex in all its musical failure.

In this poem, as in others, I am impressed by the freshness and profusion of metaphor, fortified by a quasi-surrealist technique, an invention of links and leapings that propels the poem forward without loss of momentum till its impulse is exhausted.

Now and then the element of fantasy mocks any effort at logical explanation. "The Conjurer," for example, presents a colony of tiny people diminished by magic and kept in a mayonnaise jar. The speaker, who is responsible for their condition, is irritated by their growing recalcitrance and independence. He toys with the notion of dumping them out "into a real garden" where they would be at the mercy of the voracious ants. At night, in a dream, they crawl inside his left ear with candles, exploring for his brain among the stalactites, seeking the magic spell that might release them. When he wakes, he is assailed by the disturbing memory of a trick: "Yes, a trick, I'll tell them to close / their eyes I've something for them." Only gradually do we perceive that this master of the black art is revealing to us the way he entrapped his victims at the time of their shrinking. Is it a sinister parable of psychoanalysis, as one of my friends reads it? I detect greater affinities with the story of creation, whether poetic or divine. But I do not care much whether the conjurer is to be equated with Dr. Freud or the poet or God, or . . . in his ambiguity . . . all three. What moves me is the plight of those lilliputians who are "really" trapped in that mayonnaise jar, as I am moved by all those other characters in Maura Stanton's poems who struggle to enunciate the saving word out of their nightmare predicament of dumbness, paralysis, or stuttering.

Maura Stanton did not turn to poetry till she was twenty-two. Before then she fabricated suspense novels and murder mysteries and "dreamed about exotic places when it snowed." At the University of Minnesota, while studying Latin American politics, she discovered Elisa Lynch, the 19th-century Irish adventuress who became the mistress of the dictator of Paraguay and served as a colonel in his army. The final section of this book consists of a still unfinished sequence of poems that are projected through Elisa's reckless and flaming persona. It is the kind of identification, ostensibly with one's own opposite—as, for example, John Berryman with Anne Bradstreet—that seems to lead to self-discovery and the release of hidden powers. In their controlled violence, circumambulating the fringes of hysteria, these poems are the most dramatic and accessible that Maura Stanton has written.

My ultimate impression is of a poet of snow and flame, one who conveys a sense of burning reality, of the strange fire within and without, crackling with spirit and invention. In the midst of this "tumult of perception" her poems stand separate and achieved, with deceptively cool surfaces: a delicious paradox.

STANLEY KUNITZ

I

Perspectives

One night a blunt wind
scoured my eyes for hours:
I sold Christmas seals,
ringing doorbells, holding up gold
stamps with egg-white angels
trumpeting askew in the trees.
It was heaven: a gaudy fishbowl
where the saints mooned
forever at a clay child, a bird—
for fifty cents. The houses
half crystallized in the snow,
turned blue with Christmas lights
strung in ersatz steeples
over the front-yard crèche
where a dog moved wolflike.
Years later, I found a curled
seal in a bureau crack, the angels
still shiny at resurrection.
I burned it to delicate ash
on the sidewalk, watching an ant
clamber furiously from the smoke
with a huge bread crumb
lodged in his black jaw, & thought:
"How well I understand."
Somehow today, squinting
at a file of ants on a leaf—
they're inscrutable as cuneiform.
I believed death was simply
bone against bone, thoughtlessness—

the way a crushed ant dries
 & blows through the grass
without memory or direction.
What were angels but wishes?
Now their pellucid wings
loom in my dreams. I see
the real meaning of trumpets
 & that fierce gift, not death,
but the tumult of perception.

Mykonos

Houses knuckle from the soil
in this immense light called classic:
I think of women in stone clothes.
Wind goes mad in the usual olive trees.
Goat skull on the path. Whole herds
of goat are moving on small hoofs
under my closed lids until I am black
with history. All beans and executions.
I want to be perfect, frozen
over a broken sandal; my hand
to pluck, nervous, at a strap forever,
narrow pleats flowing like rain
from a slim neck. Of course no head.
All the space behind my eyes shot off.
Tourists would say I screamed
for my lost face. A bird flicks up.
The skin on these white grapes
is tight as fingertips. The sea
flecked with shrapnel. Everything ends
in detail, chips of marble, bone, brain
cells with whole wars in their chemicals.

The Sled

Air cuts like wire
. . . left, sharp, the lake spins undangerously
away, an outer space of white field
smashes into sight, the jolt comes
up the spine shaft with its memories:
how paralysis must be water, the sand-
bar here, tide rising; no one swims
except choked as clams in the iron lungs.
Up the hill my husband waves, you're safe!
I go up. He thought I'd crack open
revealing my ivory tusk, that treasure
cached under my skin he can't touch.
At night I get afraid; his fingers probe
needlelike tracing the snaking curve
of knobs he calls talisman! good luck!
I remember polio: braces, hooks, machines
shiny as sled runners, the wool packs
steaming my body like a snowman's
Under his hand my skin thaws blue.
Is he a doctor? I want to fly
toward the lake until ice breaks me.
A survivor has white lips sucking
her brain, all those other beds
crammed with nervous children in gowns
who tumble forever in snowlight
unable to stand. Once more downhill
together, his arms saying alive! alive!
we lean from the lake & keep going.

A Voice for the Sirens

Oh they came, their eyes blank.
I pinned their souls under rocks
wanting only their shocked flesh
as the ships broke up, again, again . . .
Years now. Unlike the others I remember
a hand, some coarse hair against my cheek.
Now I stare at the sea all day
singing about strange events
for I've passed through their souls
inadvertently, thinking them shadows—
their souls were particles of odd happenings
or geography or touch,
tainting my immortality with memory.

As the sea roiled around him, one sailor
dreamed of his wife's tomb,
the steep, sweating walls & dead pigs
killed to entice away worms.
Another rubbed sea salt into his eyes
as if it were home, the desert;
while the one I murmured over, sweetly
dead in my young, implacable arms
saw his father turn in another sea.
In this fairyland, their strenuous lips
only blub loosely like the octopus
crossing my feet with lank, amorous
tentacles; their fingers dissolve
into the sharp, familiar bone.

Sometimes I hear mariner's wives chanting
over the water, like us, forlorn;
I remember the charmed wedding nights,
& each man's last embrace snow-
flake patterned into his soul, now mine.
Yet I keep singing, my dangerous voice
joined in sad irresponsibility with those
on this rock who forget why
each time until the next ship crashes.
Into the haunted music I weave my warning
carefully, as if my language were decipherable.

Dreaming of Shells

I'm never alone now.
You rise through the silver air
of upstate New York through a dream
where each raindrop turns to a minnow.
Here is the signature of your life:
a cap pulled down over your eyes
while you speak pidgin Russian
familiarly in a blue room with women
who admire the insides of shells.

I admired the conch
for all its intricate pathways
north to the white sea I imagined
from the Midwest, on front porches
where the first kiss shocked.
The mouth is a shell.
Enter at your own risk
because I've exorcised my gentleness.
My tongue is glass in this stanza.

You find glass by the sea, too,
washed smooth as shells
who believe it's a dangerous crustacean.
I'm not afraid of dark
only of what moves within it, up
steep walls into my heart.
I'll admit it, I'm my own metaphor:
You are the grain of sand
each night I translate into pearl.

Widows

Somebody's mother has arrived in snow,
her hands crooked over the reins.
The man beside her, mild & nodding,
did not believe in thermometers.
The mercury shrank his heart

until his eyes splintered, two moons
drifting invisibly in the white sky.
She has no illusions. The children
will not be home for the disturbance.
They've hung a mirror on the door

over the knocker, & she sees
dreams cross a face almost recognizable.
Who is that girl near the cradle
singing to her dark hair, that ghost
traveling backwards into her husband?

The snowflakes are the landscape's
only gesture, frosting her dark coat
dispassionately with a small chill.
The muffled jingle of her walleyed
mare startles her hands into motion.

She brushes snow from the man's warped
lip, thinking, perhaps this is the wrong
boulevard or address. But her grief-struck
daughter gapes from the upstairs window
afraid of her mother, of the stone man

brought to her house as inheritance.
"This attitude is distorted" she whispers
while her mother wipes more snow
from his iron cheek, & disappears
through monotonous streets with the sled.

The All-Night Waitress

for Gail Fischer

To tell the truth, I really *am*
a balloon, I'm only rubber, shapeless,
smelly on the inside . . .
I'm growing almost invisible.
Even the truckers admire my fine
indistinctiveness, shoving their fat hands
through my heart as they cry,
"Hey, baby! You're really weird!"
Two things may happen: if the gas
explodes at the grill some night,
I'll burst through the greasy ceiling
into black, high air,
a white something children point at
from the bathroom window at 3 A.M.
Or I'll simply deflate.
Sweeping up, the day shift will find
a blob of white substance
under my uniform by the door.
"Look," they'll say, "what a strange
unnatural egg, who wants to touch it?"
Actually, I wonder how I'd
really like being locked into orbit
around the earth, watching
blue, shifting land forever—
Or how it would feel to disappear
unaccountable in the arms of some welder
who might burst into tears
& keep my rubbery guts inside his lunch box
to caress on breaks, to sing to . . .

Still it would mean escape
into a snail's consciousness, that muscular
foot which glides a steep shell
over a rocky landscape, recording passage
on a brain so small how could it hurt?

In Ignorant Cadence

The chemical tapestry of your brain
amazes the heart of you,
all those ions & neural protons

clicking into scenes or wishes.
Your tongue is alive
in your mouth like a slippery fish

so why can't you say anything?
Even Philomela, throat stanched with rags,
managed to shred her weaving fingers

until the thread equaled
recklessness from once upon a time.
The tongue of a bird is a delicacy—

yours, a distraction you never understood,
a hopeless slab of muscle
forever wobbling on the edge of song.

Barnyard

for Flannery O'Connor

These men in full crimson
    blouses have lean
troutlike fingers in the old-time cracker

barrel, delving among gherkins
    & bulgar wheat
as if they had coins in their ears.

I place you here by the flour sacks
    wearing jeans with plaid
flannel, glum faced, your pale eyes

wincing a smile. You never put
    gypsies into a scene
but they crouched offstage

blowing their knives white.
    I catch them sometimes
at night when you ride like a hard-

breathing miner into my brain.
    I have never seen your stiff
photograph, crutches gawky as storks,

but I know why your barnyard
    was strewn with peacock feather.
The yellow wagons were camped

just past the tree line,
    harness bells too soft
for your country of stone-lipped inhabitants.

Unwell

If you dream of cancer, what cure
except to pack your heart
with snow until you turn stone?
You say your blood runs white
with small parasites. Each night
disease kisses your brain with ring-
worm, your spine freezes into ice.
You tell yourself, "you're well, well!"
but count your breaths
like angels no one else perceives.
"Isn't your skin too thin," you wonder,
"will the veins work out or spill
into bruises?" You moon at the window,
your eyes glass like a doll's,
an axle in your skull spinning
"be sweet now" or "sad."
You hold your head erect to let
the carotid shoot free into the cells
that make this imagery alive
in your speech. You believe in every nerve—
their tiny hands clap pain
until your bravery goes mute, a worn
cherub mouthless in the nave.
Something brilliant in your mind
magnifies bacteria like a microscope:
You might be insane: You won't
admit anything except imagination,
the real fever burning in your head.

Judith Recalls Holofernes

While he slept, I poured salt in his ears.
Yes, it was easy
until the wasps escaped from the first hole in his neck
to blind me with wings
settling iridescent on my arms while I hacked
fiercely into the spine.
When it was over, I kissed his lips
then thumbed the eyes open
looking for my reflection in the dark pupil.
Actually, it was my maid
wielding the sword with strong, anonymous fingers.
I hid in the sheets, imagining
how many soldiers in the mountains
north of Bethulia dreamed of me each night.
Excuse me, it's hard to remember:
the blue tent, the olives,
Holofernes leaning into my breasts
describing something called "snow."
Did he have a beard or was that Anchior?
Perhaps I poisoned him first, yes, of course.
He drank greedily, his muscles
rippling silver in the light while he pulled
my left earlobe in fun.
Let me try out your sword, I said.

His wife writes me sad letters, asking for detail.
Did he eat well? Or catch cold?
Judith, you're the heroine, she says, I can't complain

about history, but didn't he call
my name in his sleep?
I write back: I'm not sure, I think the sword
flew by itself, a miracle, into his throat.
I'm not responsible for God.

This is our shipwrecked anniversary
which I celebrate by lighting a candle
inside his skull above the town gate
except, this year, they've torn it down.
Listen, his heart simply burst—
he was singing, he was so lonely
he stuffed flowers in his mouth
just to entertain me a moment longer.
Why did he hang his sword on the bedpost?
No, I don't remember.
Something is buzzing in my head,
something that sounds like a thousand
transparent wings rising behind my eyes.

Proteus's Tale

Water touched water through my heart.
I fell into a white tangle of octopus,
fluttering for air, one molecule, one second . . .
something ghosted across my brain, fiber
or seeds rising on the black negative.
Then I fled into whales, into thread-fine
fish where I ate muscle from my own bones,
into the conch, believing I was a sea.
As sea anemone, prehensile, I waved
tentacles in the dark; crept with snails,
frightened of the impulse snapping
whatever-I-was into eels, minnows, bones,
into coins stamped with bees, into memory.
The membranes weren't sealed. I escaped—
light or energy—through mysterious windows.
Rents appeared in my insane fabric,
I'd tumble out of shape into other edges,
the cliff of my own dreams looming blue
in the shark's thrust for the swimmer.

The Snow House

I could kick down this children's igloo
in two minutes, telling them how dangerous
structures of snow can be, or merely
fall against the roof . . .
They.watch me gravely, expecting
admiration for the ice-welding
done with the garden hose for permanence.
But I remember my husband's story
recollected in irony:
how the neighbor children
sealed him in their snow fort
& when he burst through, was it
imagination? his lungs hurt—
That night I dreamed of ghostly children
passing me in a snow field.
"We have buried him!" they chanted,
melting as I ran blinded
into the white dark of a blizzard.

Remembering that dream, these children
frighten me with their innocence.
Their eyes would darken
if I described suffocation in their ice palace,
how adults fear their small fists
smashing towards them in visions
trapped like kaleidoscope designs . . .
infinite, made with a few stones.
That child in the red hat
is me, moving across the snow, singing.

Crawling inside, the blue walls
remind me of my brother's snow house
where I hid once in anger,
licking the ice until my tongue stuck.
"Let's pretend to freeze to death!" the children
shout from outside as I imagine
turning silver before their shocked eyes
the way I wanted to then, absolute
under my mother's wild hands.
Outside I wipe the frost off my cheek
praising their fierce construction.
If I kicked their snow house into snow,
I'd return each night
to build it up, flake by flake . . .

Short Story

Last night I flew a helicopter
over the flooded lowlands.
When the engine caught fire, I swam the fields,
knocking submerged tractors with my silver
finlike feet while the farm women
drowned around me, holding their children
over their heads for rescue.

I took two children on my back, but soon
they chanted, "You aren't our mother!"
& slipped under holding hands.
Later, when I saw their hair on the water,
salt lapped in my mouth: the story
was too sad for the protagonist
in the first person, who survives too late.

Below me I saw farmers
dancing against their pitchforks in a current,
eels twined in their beards.
Surely their dissolving eyes revealed catastrophe
in all its moral delight—
but my arms wheeled on; I remembered rumors
about mermaids, how they grow heartless, heartless.

In the House of the Brain

My women with insane attitudes
wallow in the white lake of the nucleus.
Smashed in my brain, they can't swim.
Still, they clap for help with blue hands,
crying, will you tell our secrets,
we tread on your face! we're drowning!
So I pull one up, her mouth stuck
on my neck, a chemical bloomed into a swan
who must go back, staring from my eyes.
The poem in the house of the brain
smells of acid. The floorboards dip
underwater while women clamber on the roof
calling to sisters who float
for trees or bits of board out of sight.
What do I rescue? I see bone
gleaming fishlike through skin, gills even,
then a collapse: some grit, a lost word.
Why aren't they grateful for water,
membrane that might close up their mouths
forever: yet they believe in air—
unable to see how it oxidizes, unable to breathe.

Poem

for Richard

I know a man who loved
only his tall shadow up the wall
because it had no eyes or mouth.
Another so lonely he danced
with bags of sugar in his arms
until the room spun white.
Perhaps it is sorrow you touch
in the dark, all the usual
mistakes flowing into my sleep
as I turn toward you, away.

Still, I've lost my sympathy
in distant confusion
where the man whose silver bones
I refused speaks sadly
to the man who mailed me snow.
They want to float me down
into affliction, into their personal
fathom in my memory
where the light's so bad I grope
for you, for you whom I love.

The Invention of Mortality

I was surprised to wake up
floundering on dry land, a normal child
with strange dreams about mermaids.
Did I wish for this transformation?
My new skin had edges I swam
up against continually; the air shocked.
A bird could peck out your eyes.
I recalled a game underwater, "gull shadow,"
where I counted each dark flicker
for prizes, odd shells, starfish.

When the scars healed on my neck
water even strangled—
I discovered how other children tumbled
ashore "dead," people said, "angels."
I thought they had stones in their throats
for they never spoke about blue
caves I couldn't reach
or the exact shade of the black coral
branching upward to trap sailors.

Then it was all clear, how I imagined
sealight in my worst dreams
because a rock could open my skull—
the chemicals would spill, blue, green,
over my amazed face.
I grew afraid of my artistry
in abstracting death, in flashing it
derisively before every kiss

where I might taste salt in wildness.
The hands of a lover brush
over my closed lids, & I remember
the old interpretations of shadow, of prize.

II

A Few Picnics in Illinois

Sometimes I hear haunted mouths
tearing at leaves or thistles
in the woods. At Starved Rock
the Indians entered their bodies
like caves, delving for rain
in the green spaces between bones.
I saw bones, later, at Dixon Mounds
where families like mine
gaped at skeletons
excavated scientifically from farmland.
At Jubilee Park, a soft fungus
licked pews in the stone church.
I couldn't grasp "a hundred years old"
& ran from a face in the wavy
glass that was me, distorted—
Once I tossed a Lincoln penny
over the tourist guardrail at a bed
in Lincoln's house, wondering
if he slept like me, legs curled
against the danger of wolves.
Oh yes I see Lincoln's ghost
down on his hands & knees
after that coin. Touching the head
like braille, he shrieks—
A Chicago woman drowned
at Starved Rock one summer:
For two weeks she made history,
the spot on the bank marked X
for children like me who imagined

her white neckbone in the weeds.
As her eye glazed, she saw
something new in the water, her body
floating away from her . . .

Elegy for Snow

My grandmother dreamed
of horses with red flanks
moving in a cloud through the village.
The riders changed into swans,
she said, & beat turbulent
over her young girl's head—
It meant travel, snow.
                              She emigrated.
My own dreams are blind, without
prophecy . . .
Sometimes she floats across them,
staring furiously with the oiled
irresponsible eyes of the dead.
I once rode the Rock Island Line
north at Christmas, watching
snow vanish ghostlike into dark.
My face rose on the window
in white fragments, disfigured with breath
freezing across the glass.
I was really a snowmaiden
melting down to strange rock
even then, kissing my grandmother
who dripped at the heart, her snowflakes
packed, designless . . .
Sometimes I light candles
for the old Irish who fiercely
outlive their bodies, insisting
on a resurrection in the hot
mouths of their children's children.

All I want is her dream, though—
those red horses signaling
movement over a continent, home
through the Illinois snow
to an imprisoned memory, not her,
but myself, myself, myself.

Letter to Kafka

Your closed eyes bulge like mushrooms.
While you sleep, I carve maps on your skin,
asking forgiveness with awkward kisses,
asking, do you understand theft, how I need
your white sperm? The fiancée
in her lace dress, jilted, arranging her mouth—
is really me—wearing a shawl of razors.
I tilt my head, telling the waistcoated suitor:
"Of course I believe in friendship!" I believe in whales.
I believe in the magic of water on the brain,
your illness, my teeth, our postponed death.
All those letters in your vest, the good wishes
scribbled by me & other eager women
they're only ransom notes, knives at our throats.

If you mumble about your father
what can I say? Here is mine—
a whole childhood of frown & circumference
locked on a prairie without history,
without oracular words like "Prague" or "Jew."
Of course you want nothing from me. You are salt.
You fly in my wounds when I wake up
blind in the darkness, calling for a thesaurus
to explain sex in all its musical failure.

Job's New Children

These perfect children sleep
with gold coins on their eyes—
they're angels, crammed unmercifully
into meager bones. Cassia, my second son,
stoops in the hall like a dwarf
flapping imaginary wings, but when I glance
at his stone-colored face
he says, "Father, I honor you,
I would kill all my ewes & rams . . ."
My snowfall daughters
watch for birds in the date palms.
They've unlatched the dovecote,
kissed each dove into flight
& moon anxiously at the king's
peacocks in bamboo cages.
At twilight I've caught them hopping
in the air like iridescent
insects near fire.
Dies, my first son, offers holocausts:
A sparkless flame eats his favorite
animals for love, but I'm
nervous under his prismatic eyes.
He wants to sacrifice his heart.
Under his wool tunic, he's traced
the priest's red circle.
Even Cornustibii, my golden one,
averts his head from the jiggling
breasts of servant girls.

I'm too old. My friends Sophar
& Baldad exclaim "What shiny
children!" awestruck at my potency.
But the seed's wrong.
These children aren't gay but holy—
like that fish born
miraculously to a starving woman
who still died, unable to eat.
I see a daughter in the garden
swinging her arms until they blur in air.
She suffocates in her skin.
She is my just reward, my blessing.

Ophelia

Each night I walk the moon, myself, strange
planet inhabited by a girl rendered backwards
by pool or mirror into the odd logic of image—
What self-deception! How could I recognize
my own ghost rising from the graveyard stream,
how could my ghost locate the narrow bones
she's never seen, or do worms mouth gossip?
Here, walking this shadowless dust, I watch
a light spin dangerous across the atmosphere;
suddenly, I'm awake, holding this man's hard
muscles in my arms, falling down on his face
until his lips suck me alive into daylight.
Yes, I'm off balance. He sees me opposite
myself, as myself isn't, calls me columbine,
sweet rose, or daisy with long arms—
If I twined myself with greens, with weeds,
he'd never discover how deep inside my thicket
I've escaped my rare womanly blooms; or how
forever I'm only the sandswept desert,
pitiless, listening to the sphere's wild music
only I can translate, but I won't! I won't!

North

*In the city of Richmond the monuments
to the heroes who survived the civil war
face south. Those who died face north.*

On Monument Avenue the dead
heroes stare north at their souls . . .
Once I drove through the traffic circle,
a blue grey statue crammed
at the edge of my new peripheral vision.
The driving instructor cried "Careful" as a moth
unraveled on the windshield
startling my hands off the wheel: I balanced
north, the green wings blowing up
"Luna" somewhere inside, & the red light.
"So you plan to drive north," the man muttered
& I remembered winters when I saw
my soul as white breath
sucked glacially from my body.
That night I dreamed of Jeb Stuart
clawing snow off a river
only to find the ice opaque. No reflection.
Now I imagine him unhistorically
crossing tundra, leading a snow-blind horse
with messages for the other generals on Monument . . .
When a strange explosion cut power, I saw ghost troops
hovering in the sudden woods of the city.
I lit a candle for fugitives in every window.
"Here is the north!" I waved wildly
out at the darkness, at the moon
snared in the webs of the radio tower.
I wanted to drive some exhausted
soldier home with me, north up the freeways

state by state, watching his heart
spread over his tunic like a miracle.
"It's Illinois, we're getting close," I'd whisper
while his eyes stumbled black.
"In Minnesota, your blood won't flow . . ."

Grandfather

You slept evenly, hardly rumpling the sheet.
Later, I thought of places in Tennessee. The green
leapt off those hills, you said, explaining
your apple-core eyes.
A white field rumpled your jaw at night,
growing its own winter
carefully, without waste of time.
Sometimes you counted the acres
you never owned, over and over, on fingers
handcuffed with age; you squinted
hospital fern into trees. How could
I know your sorrow? It was so private,
locked behind your fine, half-Cherokee skull,
and almost over, your face
tangled as the map of a civilized country.

Caring for the Generals

Was it warm rubbing
vaseline on their wiry chests, holding
their wrists like the necks of limp
geese? Was their skin
covered with metal stars?
I see them flapping
up the corridor in starched nightshirts,
their hernias bandaged, yelling
for apples and fresh lettuce.
They bathe in bright tin containers
that whirl the water until
it is nearly milk. When the mechanized
sound shuts off and buzz bombs
skim uneasily into London,
they are in the basement
spinning wheelchairs, betting
on the nearness of the explosion.

The Conjurer

In a mayonnaise jar I keep the tiny
people I shrank with my magic; I didn't
know they'd hold each other's hands & cry
so sharply when I said, no, the spell's
irreversible, do you eat grass or breadcrumbs?
Two are lovers who claim the air's bad
down there, & bite my fingers when I offer
a ride. They don't understand me.
I keep the jar by a window, washing
soot off the glass walls periodically . . .
When I gave them a flower, some ants
in the stamen attacked viciously,
gnawing the man-in-the-fur-cap's leg
completely off, while the others squealed
at the punched lid for his rescue:
I thumbed the ant dead, but were they grateful?
Lately they've begun to irritate me,
refusing raw meat, demanding more privacy
as if they were parrots who need cage covers
for daytime sleep. The awkward lovers
break apart at my shadow, nonchalant . . .
They're weaving something out of grass,
a blanket maybe, growing thin to save
their stalks, eating only breadcrumbs.
Don't they see? I could dump them
out into a real garden, let them tunnel
through the weeds to an anthill.
One night I dreamed those lovers crawled
inside my left ear with candles,

trying to find my brain in a fog.
They moved deep among the stalactites
searching for the magic spell they thought
I'd lost in sleep. I knew better.
Still, I woke with something resurrected
in my memory, maybe only a trick,
yes, a trick, I'll tell them to close
their eyes I've something for them.

Elegy for the Whole Ward

Your heart tumbles like the ocean
trapped in a conch: all those wires
waxed to your bare chest listen
for strangling thickets of blood or low tide.
We call this "near death" & can't see
any difference. A sudden glaze of eye,
the needle jerky, then steady, a compass
pointing due north or where? You still
breathe. These signs don't amaze us yet.
Under the oxygen mask, if you feel rime
kissing your brain, nothing distracts
from the freeze: your wife can't.
The nurses arrange your pliable bratwurst
hands, rolling your sleeve to get vein
for glucose bottles on wire hatracks.
Imagine, you have a stomach, teeth,
feet, a heartbeat, other organs that go!—
But you don't know what's happening, not
even the way a snail knows about danger
& sand lice: You can't rage.
Everything's sliced from your memory
so what's left? Your lungs gutter
up & down, the sheet moves: the doctor
mutters "not gone" as if he saw you.

The Boy Next Door: A Pastoral

A prince can wed the Sleeping Beauty or
someone even harder to win, but the Sleeping
Beauty can be no prince.   —Kafka

1   *The Hymen*

The shepherdess meets the grimy boy
lifting her dresden over the stile
where he whistles, "Lady! The sun & moon!"

Then he throws a rose. Her glass face
breaks open: all the rough bits amaze him!

So women are made of rubbage! He glues
each shattered crevice with a kiss.

★

But this is some centuries later,
she thinks, fucking in the back seat,
her fingers hardened to thimbles.
She is held together with pins.
He pulls them out, one by one by one

until she plays rock to his paper, every game,
only dreaming of scissors.

Of course there is always wine
standing in stone jars: the blossoms,
the guests, even that strange-eyed wizard

blessing the leavened bread & children.
Under her white dress, the old semen
keeps her skin moving toward skin,

the only direction she ever wished for,
her breasts growing easy as yeast
under the hands of a real love.

And now the old enemy, vanquished.
Never to sleep alone, the emptiest space
filled with flesh & blood forever.

The Fisherman's Wife

The fisherman said I was his third wish.
He washed off the salt, taught me to breathe,
kick my scissory legs & doze
trembling in the sharp straw beside him.
Now he had boots, a boat, a wife with gill-
silver skin who peered at the sky for fish.
I couldn't speak: The nets in my throat
trapped the shiny movements of words;
the new hands, glimmering in the dark,
only stuttered like ice across his back
while I gulped for the water! the water!
needing the density of his mouth.
When I mended sails, the needle pricked
seawater from my veins; the other wives
scurried out of their clogs for the priest
who rubbed me with garlic against the devil.
A pelican dipped & angled for my eyes—
yet I couldn't drown; the angry water
shoved me into the light, I washed inland,
shellfish clamped in my streaming hair.
The fisherman plucked leeches from my neck,
crying, "You're the last wish!" I saw torn
boots, the boat shattered on a rock.
I dreamed I was out at sea, but the shapes
went blue, blurred, I wasn't anything,
a chill, a wish, his wife stirring in sleep.

The Goosegirl

Imagine these geese—
how lice rave in the hulls of their feathers
infecting even you, your golden hair
tied up with black bootstring.
Under your fingernails, lice nibble.
Aren't you ashamed of those ruddy welts
crossing your neck?
When the prince arrives, hide in a thicket.
He will hunt your geese, calling: "Crows! White Crows!
All good fortune!"

Rumors of golden eggs
crop up in market gossip—
Should you flee the kingdom,
luring your geese with breadcrumbs?
The prince gallops in pursuit,
promising keepsakes, gilt brushes & bathtubs,
even a flock of swans!
All he wants: that swarm of dirty poultry
sniveling around your ankles.
"Lady! Please!" He offers half-a-kingdom.
You say, "And my hair?
Do you love my golden hair?"
He nods, disemboweling a goose
before your wrenched eyes with a pocketknife.

Going Back

The only whistle now is something odd
stuck in your brain: you haven't lived so long
you don't need ghosts. That ex-con who robbed
the mail from Cortland isn't dead, they say:
for eighty years he's combed the Erie–Lackawanna yard
for gold or rings his women never wore.
Today the rusted tracks go straight to Homer,
three miles down. No bridge blew up. No flood
wiped out the valley. The chalk red station
glowers in the sun but no train rumbles:
you kick at bits of stained-glass transom,
wondering where he sleeps. The boxcars
remind you this is home, the corset factory
making steel ball bearings, the St. Charles Hotel
crammed with old men who watch the tracks:
who won't believe in ghosts except themselves.

Maybe he sleeps in the stationmaster's
cabin. The boards peel white.
You wonder how he stands this light, grubbing for gold
that gets scarcer, that never was there.
The thing he died for burns alive.
You want it. You want a crime bigger than any
life you might waste, bigger than any hometown.
Across the tracks the bums curl up in oil drums;
no freights to jump, you wonder where they came from,
how they go. Your skull's intact, the skin
unbroken over lute-shaped bones.
You wonder if you're turning ghost yourself,
haunting your past like snow on snow.

The Stutterer

The invention of a mountain
shouldn't surprise you: or, blue hotels
crammed with fake bannisters . . .
Sometimes you forget.
On the prairie, snow inhabits your eyes.
You imagine sod huts to crawl under,
telling yourself, "The Swiss dissemble."
The neighbors feed you sugar like a cripple,
whispering at the clothesline
about the worms nuzzling your throat.
Hissing, words have no edge.

Nothing escapes logic.
Eat salt until your lips
burn white. Try to yell "Wolf!"
while your heart cracks in its ribcage.
Nobody runs. Aren't your eyes bad?
You want to dig your way to China
where women chalk their skin.

There's no hope.
Each sentence curls into lies
spidery as asters. You call your father
a waterclock, thinking all is explained . . .
Who understands? You grow silent,
ekeing the words from a tundra of stubborn cells.

Lovers Leaving My Bed

Lumbering in the dark for shoes
or underwear, they find the car keys
with their toes & say goodnight,

can't sleep here, too unsafe,
going a little crazy tonight & besides
insomnia may be coming like a light.

If the sheet stays warm
for half-an-hour, why do I dream
avalanche! & wake unscreaming

aware of the glacial movements
of whole centuries? Nothing can stop
these lovers from leaving my bed

too soon, mumbling of work & guilt,
kisses like bald dandelions.
Even at midnight speech has no

touch or pity when the door slams—
like the fat, blue coins of archeology
paid out for brides long ago.

The Dreams

My husband says he's lost
his lips or hands somewhere
on my breasts & wants them back.
I offer dreams: he's trapped
inside my diamond cells, his kiss
or gesture floating up disguised as blue
rock or father. His genitals touch off chemicals
called "joy" but I can't wait
for sleep, going under, my mouth stuck
bloodless on his cheek.
My swan-eyed children poke tiny
fists inside my eyelids—
burrowing into my imagination,
why are they changed to dead lightning
bugs, their glow permanent?
I feed these dreams, luring them
from mineral where they prog water
into my light, whispering, eat out my eyes!
Waking up, skin pebbled with salt,
I can't talk: while I go blind
at the heart, they fade
as if I were a television, blank
& snowy, a screen for their comedy
called "My Death" in a thousand acts.

Autobiography

In your autobiography I'm the ibex
with white recurved horns
tossing in the thin mountain air.
You mention my survival tactic,
how I learned to breathe
snow at high altitudes
then pass on to the sad women
you kept leaving in chapter five.

In chapter eight, I think
you've planned to discover me in ice
frozen with wild hysterical eyes.
"Oh, she's climbing the precipice,"
your researchers whisper;
"she'll illuminate your middle age
with the dead's irony."

You love that room of mirrors
where everything's complex
except your simple women
who sing back your autobiography
over and over on tape, adding
metaphors for your loneliness.
"Tell me about the ibex," you say.
The voices spin on, inventing
my hoofs, my fine hair, my love
of risk on dark, inviolate trails . . .

If I become your fiction
of course I'll plunge
downward with the avalanche.
I've seen it all on film,
the graceful, upright hoofs
turning silver among the snowflakes.
The ignorant tribesmen arrive, shaggy—
it's the next century—to worship
this strange extinct ibex
imprisoned deep in a blue wall.
Then the snow shifts, the crevice
disappears into the mountain.

III

Extracts from the Journal of Elisa Lynch

*Elisa Lynch was the Irish mistress
of Francisco Solano Lopez, dictator
of Paraguay from 1862 to 1870. She
was a colonel in his army during the
war with Argentina, Brazil, and Uruguay
in which Lopez and her oldest son
were killed. She died in Paris.*

1. May, 1866

Distance doesn't matter, Francisco,
nothing matters, not cigars, yerba maté,
brandy stanching the pain of black teeth.
The violent garden was always lush soil.
The Guaraní girl, naked & mad in the shrubs
is really me tugging at your genitals.
Let's put away detail, your height, my hair
limned grey at the nape & all language
stuffed manic into song or thesaurus.
Skin is the only safe country; defies
even my nightmare of beached whales
rotted to white ghost ships on the Chaco.
The route across anywhere is scrub forest
gaudy with snakes & headhunters. How could
we survive alone? No trails, no water,
no mapped skies, instinct or destination.

2. December, 1868

The donkeys bray in the ditches, legs broken,
straw twisted in their eyes: I killed two men
yesterday; I am not changed into a lizard
although the Guaraní have a wooden cage, two thin
mice for my dinner. They look at my fingers for scales
or the green mold which sprouts from my heart.
Last night, Francisco, wasn't my skin odd
under your fingers? My words gagged me,
feathers, feathers . . . you said I was Lot's salt
wife, immobile except for a brain like blue light.
So death is boring. See, it comes rigid lipped,
too small for hell, celebrated by these blind
donkeys who gnaw their riders. "A woman who kills
will eat sand like the lizard." Isn't my throat
dry? Do you believe my knees are fattening?
A lizard crawls on the battlefield, alive
& blinking over rocks, over the hands of soldiers.

3.   March, 1870

Horseback. Over the Chaco.
Yesterday we found the mining
engineer haphazard in sand.
A hundred gaudy butterflies
sucked & swirled on his skin.
I said, Francisco, those flowers . . .
Today the mistress of Paraguay
lost grey gloves, her first born,
Pancho. A silver pain—
clean as any compass needle
jabbed through the heart of a mutineer.
Already landscape grows internal.
Asunción tilts on its hill, off-angle,
fragile as cigarette paper. Lopez
they mock me: Madame General!
My nipples hum under linen.
My bastard children claw
for the enemy's Argentine sugar cane.
Look, already their eyes burrow.
I want to tell them secrets,
whisper magic words for keepsakes
until we all disappear. These lessons
grow difficult, the map not parchment
& blotted ink but our own soil,
the firstborn's heart open, flowery—
(the Indian women, cleverer,
ate their husband's sperm & intentions.)
Lizards flick, usual over flat rock.
The war subsides. Madame General

breakfasts on spoiled avocado,
counting her children like lemmings.
How do I teach erratic geography,
sudden snow in the ruined vineyards?
Nothing to make it worth telling, only
roots in a damp cellar gone beserk
through the walls for our oxygen.

4. March, 1870

Jungle encroaches on the veranda,
monkey-weed smelling of piss & rotten
soldiers left for the general burial.
Paraguay collapses into straw & arson.
The guards boil jacaranda with lizard
& pork salt. I tear old cloth,
dream I am hidden in mesquite
with all my silver hairbrushes & children,
straw hampers, beef, & your photograph.
Still no word. Maybe you are blind,
raving for me on bloody ankles
screaming, "O Muerte! O Meurte!
O Meurte!" I want to bandage my eyes.
Mad dogs ravage the hills. They watch
our throats, quiver, aware of civilizations,
how they end with shard & survivors.

5. November, 1875

I'm afraid of the bones swimming up
through my children's skin, the white sheen
on their lips as they gobble from tin
plates: In exile I haggle over the *ficelle*
or *petit pain*, wrap my stunned head
in vinegar cloth. Francisco, in dreams now
I bring water for your black tongue. I touch
your cheek until the silver maggots run.
Your grimace bristles in stone at Notre Dame
where I force the children to chant Guaraní
prayers to the lizard at a side altar.
Squinting at needles in dark rooms,
I blanch like a toad, thumbs flat & sore
as an old crone in a fairy tale.
No proper death, Francisco, no bullet
smashing my angry heart into shock;
only the usual butcher's crablike mouth
gnawing mine, mumbling, "You love it! Admit
you love it!" A woman's face disappears
in adversity, going under like battle
terrain with a few scrub pine left blooming,
my eyes, frightening the children on nights
when I tear off my nightgown, crying
"Look at me! Look at your mother!"